SUSHI

All about sushi	3
How to make sushi rice	4
How to fillet fish	6
How to shape sushi	8
Sushi utensils & condiments	10
Toppings for sushi	11
Nigiri sushi (seafood)	12
Nigiri sushi (egg)	14
Wrapped sushi	16
Thin rolled sushi	18
Thick rolled sushi	22
California roll	24
Hand rolled sushi	26
Sushi pockets	30
Scattered raw fish sushi	32
Scattered vegetable sushi	34
Scattered raw fish & vegetable sushi	38
Sushi wrapped in thin omelette	40
Pressed sushi	44
Western style sushi	46
Guide to ingredients	48

Published by: Cross Media Ltd.
13 Berners Street, London W1T 3LH, UK
Tel: 020-7436-1960   Fax: 020-7436-1930

Project Manager: Kazuhiro Marumo
Editor: J.L.Rollinson
Designer: Misa Watanabe
Photographer: Naomi Igawa, Hiroshi Mitani
Recipes: Nobuko Motohashi
Chef: Miyoko Yoshimura (Akasha Cooking School)
Sushi Chef: Kenichi Kobayashi
Coordinator: Masahiko Goto. Thanks to: Akasha Tōkōdō & Sono Aoki

ISBN 1-897701-82-9
Printed in Japan

All about Sushi

The most popular Japanese food

Around 2000 years ago the Japanese began preserving fish by salting it and packing it in rice. The rice was later discarded and only the fish eaten. Methods of fermentation evolved and vinegar was introduced to the rice. In time people developed a taste for both the raw fish and the vinegared rice. Sushi is basically seafood laid on top of cooked vinegared rice. Nigiri-Sushi is perhaps the best known, and originated in Tokyo in the 1800's. Sushi is widely recognised as a low calorie health food. In fact, the seafood ingredients used for the toppings and fillings contain a lot of nutrients. Tuna for example, is good for counteracting fatigue, and preventing brittle bone disease; octopus is effective in preventing arteriosclerosis and high blood pressure, and shellfish have been found to be beneficial in preventing anaemia and calming the nerves. Salmon roe is useful in alleviating various skin problems.

How to make Sushi Rice

The secret of good sushi rice is vinegar & sugar by the right measure

To make sushi rice, add vinegar to the cooked rice while it is hot, mixing it with care so that the rice doesn't become too sticky. Adjust the amount of vinegar to taste. It is advisable to use less sugar in the rice when making seafood sushi, as this will give the rice a lighter flavour.

for 450g rice

450g Japanese rice

630ml water

[A]

4 tbsp Japanese vinegar

2 tbsp sugar

¾ tsp salt

1 Wash the rice and drain it. Cook the rice and expect this sushi rice to be less wet than usual as the recipe uses 60ml less water than that in ordinary rice preparation.

2 Place the cooked rice in a flat-bottomed bowl. Mix A well, and pour it over the surface of the rice.

4

3 Mix the rice swiftly with a flat wooden spatula, but not mashing it, just allowing the vinegar contact with all of the rice. Use your strength evenly when you handle the wooden spatula, and when mixing the rice, move the spatula as if scooping the rice rather than blending it.

4 Cool the rice down swiftly by using a paper fan, and gently turning the rice with the wooden spatula. Fanning the rice prevents it from being overly sticky, and it also adds lustre.

Tip! To prevent the cooled sushi rice from drying out, cover it with a damp tea towel.

How to fillet fish

Preparation is the key:

Preparing fish for filleting varies on the kind of fish, but the most basic guidelines are: rub the scales off both sides from the tail to the head using the wrong side of a knife at a slight angle to the fish. Then chop off the head, and cut the fish open from one end to the other through the belly, gut it, and rinse it thoroughly with water.

1 Place the washed fish, with its tail to your left, and the belly facing you. Place the knife inside the belly and slide the knife towards the tail, keeping the knife close to and parallel to the inner bones, and cut out the belly.

2 Holding the cut belly side with your left hand, cut open the whole dorsal side of the fish, angling the knife close to and parallel to the inner bones, and disjoint the boned side of the fillet.

3 Place the boned side of the fillet with its tail to your right, and the dorsal side facing you. Place the knife through the dorsal fin, and slide it towards the head, angling the knife close to and parallel to the inner bones, to make a slit towards the centre of the fillet.

4 Cut from the tail towards the centre of the fillet. Raise the knife to cut out the bones. Slide the knife from the tail towards the head while the knife is close to and parallel with the inner bones to remove the fillet from the bone.

 Tip! When removing the guts, clean the fish on the inside as well as the outside, do this with running water and by rubbing the insides with your fingers.

How to shape sushi

Shaping the rice without losing the freshness of the topping

Preparation is the key:

Before you shape sushi, prepare some vinegared water (3 tbsps Japanese vinegar to 240ml water), use this to wet your hands to prevent the rice from sticking to them while shaping. Slice the toppings thinly, and grate the *wasabi* (Japanese horseradish). To shape the sushi well, without compromising the freshness of the toppings, prepare all the ingredients before you begin shaping.

1 Wet your hands thoroughly with vinegared water.

2 Lay the topping over the fingers of your left hand (palm up).

3 Take a bite size amount of sushi rice in your right hand and mould it gently into the shape of a ship's hull. While holding the sushi rice, take some *wasabi* with the index finger and place it in the centre of the topping.

4   Place the sushi rice on the topping.

5   Adjust the shape of the sushi rice.

6   Turn the sushi upside down on your left hand, so that the topping rests on top of the rice, and pinch both sides of the sushi rice with your right thumb and index finger to finish shaping it.

Tip!   The initial shaping of the sushi rice shouldn't be too firm.

Sushi Utensils & Condiments

Making sushi at home

There are quite a few traditional utensils especially for making sushi, and although you get the best results using these, they are not absolutely essential, and can substituted by quite ordinary kitchen equipment.

Sushi Utensils

❶ *Handai* (wooden bowl) —————— to mix rice & sushi vinegar
❷ *Makisu* (bamboo rolling mat) — to make rolled sushi
❸ *Uchiwa* (paper fan) —————— to cool the rice
❹ *Shamoji* (flat wooden spoon) — to stir cooked rice

Sushi Condiments

❶ *Shoyu* (Japanese soy sauce) —————— to dip sushi in
❷ *Wasabi* (Japanese horseradish) —————— used in sushi preparation
❸ *Gari* (pickled ginger) —————— sliced ginger in sweetened vinegar

Toppings for sushi

Toppings for Nigiri-Zushi

Popular toppings in Japan include:
1. Red fish such as tuna, bonito, and swordfish
2. White fish such as sea bream, turbot, and sea bass
3. Oily fish such as medium sized gizzard shad, mackerel, and sardines
4. Shellfish such as ark shell, scallop, and abalone
5. Crustacea such as prawn, crab, and mantis crab
6. Fish eggs such as sea urchin, salmon roe, and herring roe.
7. Squid and octopus are also favourites.

Sushi with originality

For other kinds of sushi such as rolled sushi and vegetable scattered sushi, which are frequently made at home, cucumber, dried strips of gourd, *shiitake* mushroom, sweet omelette, *natto* (fermented soy beans), and canned tuna are commonly used. Sushi is made of white vinegared rice, which goes well with any kind of topping, so you can feel free to experiment with a wide variety of ingredients. There are basically no rules in choosing the ingredients for sushi.

Nigiri Sushi (fish, shrimp, shellfish)
にぎり寿司 *Nigiri-zushi* ●

* See page 4 how to make sushi rice
* See page 6 how to fillet fish

Serves 1
(2 of each kind)

250g sushi rice
(25g per sushi)

40g tuna
(20g per sushi)

30g sea bream
(15g per sushi)

2 slices ark shell

2 slices scallop

2 shrimp

some Japanese vinegar

1 Slice the tuna and sea bream diagonally (6-7cm length, 3cm width).

2 Devein and skewer the shrimp. Parboil the shrimps in salted water for 30-60 seconds. Remove the skewers, shell them and slit open the undersides. Dip them briefly in the vinegar before placing them on the sushi rice.

3 Rub the ark shells in salt and rinse them with water to remove stickiness. Rinse the scallops in salted water and wipe them. To make the sushi follow the instructions on page 8.

Nigiri Sushi (Egg)

卵にぎり *Tamago-nigiri*

* See page 4 how to make sushi rice

Makes 4 sushi

100g sushi rice

4 eggs (medium)

some sunflower or vegetable oil

[A]

60ml soup stock

1 tsp light soy sauce

½ tsp salt

2 tsp sugar

1 Add A to the beaten eggs and mix well.

2  Coat a frying pan thinly with oil and pour in a small quantity of the egg mixture. When the mixture starts to swell, press it to flatten. When the mixture is half cooked, roll it towards the front of the pan. Slide the roll to the other end and pour another small quantity of egg mixture into the bare part but allowing it to ease under the cooked egg roll. Repeat the rolling procedure, adding the egg mixture until it is used up.

3 Mould the cooked egg inside a bamboo rolling mat, shaping it evenly into a rectangle. Slice it into pieces (1cm width), and make up the sushi following the instructions on page 8.

Wrapped Sushi

軍艦巻き *Gunkan-maki*

Makes 6 sushi

150g sushi rice
(25g for each sushi)

6 x sheet dried seaweed
(8cm x 2.5cm)

2 tbsp fresh tuna

2 tbsp salmon roe

2 tbsp sea urchin

1 spring onion

* See page 4 how to make sushi rice

1 Shape sushi rice as you would for normal *nigiri-zushi*.

2 Wrap the dried seaweed around the side of the shaped sushi and secure the edges with a crushed grain of rice.

3

Place tuna, salmon roe, and sea urchin on each of the shaped sushi individually and garnish the tuna ones with chopped spring onion.

Thin Rolled Sushi

● 細巻き *Hoso-maki* ●

The thin sushi roll was invented earlier than *nigiri
-zushi* (shaped sushi). Experiment with the filling
depending on your taste.

Makes 2 rolls

140g Sushi rice

25g cucumber

20g gourd
(cut in ribbons)

1 sheet dried seaweed
(21cm x 19cm)

↓

* See page 4 how to make sushi rice

1 Cut the cucumber lengthways
into eighths. Rinse the gourd,
rub it with salt, soak it in
lukewarm water and then boil
it for 4-5 minutes. Place the
boiled gourd and A in a pan,
bring to a boil, then lower the
heat and cook for 10-15 minutes.

[A]
475ml soup stock
2 tbsps sugar
2 tbsps soy sauce
1 tbsp *mirin*

2  Cut the seaweed sheet in half lengthways, and place it on a bamboo rolling mat, spread 70g rice over the sheet leaving 1cm free on the side opposite you. Lay the cucumber or gourd down the centre.

3 Place your thumbs at the back of the mat and lift it whilst supporting the filling with the rest of your fingers. Roll the rice away from you and press lightly.

. . . .

Tip!

To make a neat roll, spread the rice more thinly where the filling is to go.

4 Roll the sushi so that the edge of the dried seaweed is placed under the rolled sushi.

5

Shape the sushi by pressing each end of the roll, and cut it into 6 pieces. Repeat the process for the other filling.

Thick Rolled Sushi
● 太巻き *Futo-maki* ●

* See page 4 how to make sushi rice

Makes 1 roll

230g sushi rice

20g gourd
(cut in ribbons)

2 slices rolled omelette

¼ cucumber
(cut in quarters
lengthways)

1 grilled eel
(sliced 1cm width)

1 sheet dried seaweed
(21cm × 19cm)

1 Boil gourd according to page18. Make rolled omelette according to page14, and slice - 1cm width.

2 Place the sheet of dried seaweed on a bamboo rolling mat. Spread the rice over ¾ of the sheet, leaving 1cm free on the near side and more on the opposite side.

3 Place all the fillings down the centre and roll the sushi according to page19, then cut the roll into 8 pieces.

22

California Roll

カリフォルニア巻き *California-maki*

* See page 4 how to make sushi rice

Serves 1

230g sushi rice
½ avocado
4 crab sticks
½ cucumber
1 sheet dried seaweed
(21cm x 19cm)
2 tbsp mayonnaise
2 tbsp flying fish roe

1 Cut the skinned and stoned avocado and cucumber in quarters lengthways.

2 Spread the sushi rice over the sheet of seaweed, and sprinkle the fish roe over the surface. Place a sheet of cling film on the worktop, and turn the layer of seaweed and sushi rice upside down flat on the cling film so that the seaweed ends up on top.

3

Place the avocado, cucumber and crab sticks evenly down the centre, and coat the filling with mayonnaise. Roll the layer up from one edge, and slice the roll into 8.

Hand Rolled Sushi

● 手巻き寿司 *Temaki-zushi* ●

This is a very relaxed way of enjoying sushi and a great idea for a party, with everyone helping themselves to rice and toppings and having a go at making their own sushi.

Serves 4

800g sushi rice

8-10 sheets of dried seaweed, cut into quarters (adjust according to the number of sushi)

120g raw tuna

a few chives

* See page 4 how to make sushi rice

1. Chop up the raw tuna and mix it with the finely chopped chives. (This will make a *negitoro* roll)

. . . .

1 packet of *natto* (50g)

4 *umeboshi*

4 *shiso*

1 can of tuna

some Japanese mustard

some soy sauce

some mayonnaise

2 Stone and crush the *umeboshi*, chop the *shiso* into fine strips and mix them together. (This will make an *umeboshi* roll)

3 Stir the *natto* well, mix it with a small amount of mustard and soy sauce. (This will make a *natto* roll)

27

Tip!

You can roll sushi with salad leaves instead of seaweed.

You can use other fillings such as *takuan*, cucumber, rolled omelette, thinly sliced ham or cheese.

4 Remove the oil from the canned tuna, and mix it with mayonnaise. (This will make a tuna-mayonnaise roll)

5 Serve the sushi rice in a large bowl, and lay out the fillings and the dried seaweed on plates for people to help themselves.

6

Each person scoops up enough rice for 3-4 bites (about 60g), places it on a sheet of dried seaweed, adds the topping of their choice and rolls it up to eat.

Sushi Pockets

稲荷寿司 *Inari-zushi*

720g sushi rice

10 thin fried bean curd
(each 20g)

[A]

350ml soup stock

4 tbsp soy sauce

2 tbsp sugar

2 tbsp *mirin*

* See page 4 how to make sushi rice

1   Cut the fried bean curd into halves, and carefully open them out like pouches. Boil them in water for 2-3 mins.

2   Mix A. Drain the bean curd and pour A into the pan, cover with a lid and bring it to the boil. Once boiled, lower the heat and cook for 10 minutes until most of the sauce has evaporated.

3   Holding the pouches open gently, fill them with sushi rice. Close the opening and ease the pouch into a pillow shape.

30

Scattered Raw Fish Sushi
● 生ちらし *Nama-chirashi* ●

* See page 4 how to make sushi rice

Serves 1

250g sushi rice

some *wasabi*

[Toppings]

3 slices tuna
(20g each)

2 slices sea bream
(15g each)

1 ark shell

1 scallop

1 shrimp

1 slice squid

2 slices
rolled omelette

1 Pour 70ml hot water over the squid to parboil, and prepare the seafood following the instructions on page 12.

2 Make the rolled omelette following the instructions on page 14, and cut 2 × 3cm width slices.

3 Arrange all the toppings on the rice and serve in a bowl, garnish with *wasabi*. This dish is eaten with chopsticks.

Scattered Vegetable Sushi

五目寿司 *Gomoku-zushi*

A traditional Japanese party dish made with a very healthy combination of ingredients.

* See page 4 how to make sushi rice

Serves 4

800g sushi rice
6 *shiitake* mushrooms
20g gourd
60g lotus root
60g burdock root
60g carrot
3 eggs
4 tbsp toasted white sesame seeds

1 Place the *shiitake*, stems removed, gourd (cooked according to page 18), and A in a pan; bring to the boil then lower the heat and cook for 15 minutes. Cut the cooked *shiitake* into 5mm cubes. Cut the cooked gourd into strips, 1cm.

1 sheet dried seaweed
(21cm x 19cm)

some red pickled ginger

some sunflower
or vegetable oil

½ tsp salt

[A]

100ml soup stock

4 tbsp sugar

3 tbsp soy sauce

1 tbsp *mirin*

[B]

3 tbsp Japanese vinegar

1 ½ tbsp sugar

⅓ tsp salt

[C]

100ml soup stock

2 tsp sugar

1 tbsp soy sauce

1 tbsp *mirin*

some salt

2 Peel the lotus root, cut it in half and slice one half to reveal it's floral impression. Cut the other half lengthways in quarters, and then cut each quarter very finely (3mm width). Soak all of the root  in vinegared water to remove harshness. Boil the flower shaped lotus root for 2 minutes and then marinate in B.

3 Wash the burdock root and scrub off the skin. Shave-cut the burdock root with a knife. Peel the carrots and cut into strips, 3cm x 2 mm.

4 Heat the oil in a pan and fry the burdock root, carrot, and the finely chopped lotus root. When cooked, add C and continue cooking until the sauce is reduced to nothing.

. . . .

Tip!

Mix the rice and other ingredients 'lightly' with a wooden spatula to avoid crushing the rice.

5 Beat the eggs gently with a pinch of salt, and pour a small amount into a heated, lightly oiled frying pan to make a thin sheet of omelette. Make a few sheets, roll them on a chopping board and cut into very fine strips, 2mm.

6

Mix the sushi rice with the *shiitake*, gourd, burdock root, carrot, finely chopped lotus root and toasted sesame seeds, and serve on a plate. Garnish with the flower shaped lotus root, strips of omelette, dried seaweed and red pickled ginger.

Scattered Raw Fish and Vegetable Sushi
● ばら寿司 *Bara-zushi* ●

Serves 4

800g sushi rice
200g grilled eel
200g salmon roe
12 shrimp
3 eggs
8 mangetout
some trefoil
(to garnish)
1 sheet dried seaweed
(21cm x 19cm)
4 tbsp toasted white
sesame seeds

* See page 4 how to make sushi rice

1 Slice up the grilled eel into 2cm × 2cm strips whilst hot. Boil and shell the shrimps.

2

Beat the eggs gently, add a pinch of salt, and pour a small amount into a heated, lightly oiled frying pan to make a thin sheet of omelette. Make a few sheets, roll them on a chopping board and cut into very fine strips, 2mm. Boil the mangetout and trefoil only briefly (to retain their fresh colour), and slice into strips, 2cm. Cut the dried seaweed into thin strips.

3 Serve the sushi rice in a bowl and sprinkle with the toasted sesame seeds. Arrange the eel, salmon roe, omelette strips, moungetout, shrimp, dried seaweed and trefoil on the rice.

Sushi Wrapped in Thin Omelette

茶巾寿司 *Chakin-zushi*

This sushi is popular with children and is full of healthy ingredients.

* See page 4 how to make sushi rice

Serves 4

800g sushi rice
6 *shiitake* mushrooms
25g gourd
60g lotus root
60g burdock root
60g carrot
6 eggs

1. Place the stemmed *shiitake* and gourd (cooked according to page 18) in a pan with A, and bring to the boil, lower the heat and cook for 15 minutes. Cut the *shiitake* into 5mm cubes, and the gourd into strips, 10cm.

Chakin-zushi

. . . .

⅓ tsp salt

⅓ tsp sugar

some vegetable
or sunflower oil

[A]

100ml soup stock

4 tbsp sugar

3 tbsp soy sauce

1 tbsp *mirin*

[B]

100ml soup stock

2 tsp sugar

1 tbsp soy sauce

1 tbsp *mirin*

pinch of salt

2 Cut the lotus root finely
and quater the slices.

3

Wash the burdock root, scrub
off the skin and cut it into
shavings. Peel the carrot and
cut it into strips 3cm x 2 mm.

4 Heat the oil in a pan and fry the lotus root, burdock root,
and carrot. When tender, add B and cook until the sauce is
reduced to nothing.

5 Mix the sushi rice with the *shiitake*, gourd, lotus root, burdock root, and carrot.

6 Beat the eggs gently with the sugar and salt, and pour a small amount into a heated, lightly oiled frying pan to make a thin sheet of omelette. Make several sheets.

7

Place some sushi rice in the centre of the omelette and fold it up like gift-wrapping, and tie it with a strip of gourd.

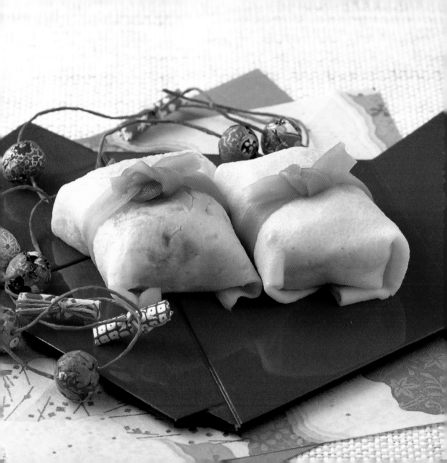

Pressed Sushi

押し寿司 *Oshi-zushi*

* See page 4 how to make sushi rice

Makes 1 roll

280g sushi rice

2 eels,
cooked & seasoned

25g *shiitake* mushrooms

[A]

100ml soup stock

4 tbsp sugar

3 tbsp soy sauce

1 tbsp *mirin*

[B]

50ml soy sauce

50ml *mirin*

25g brown sugar

1 Bring the stemmed *shiitake* and A to a boil then lower the heat; cover with a lid and cook for 15 minutes. Cut into tiny cubes.

2  Place the eel in a loose-bottomed, rectangular tin. Half fill the tin with sushi rice and press it down then sprinkle with the *shiitake* and add the rest of the sushi rice and press it all down firmly.

3 Boil B and reduce it to thicken, turn the sushi out of the box or tin upside-down to reveal the eel on top and coat the eel with B.

Western Style Sushi

洋風寿司 Yōfū-zushi

Serves 4

800g sushi rice

12 slices smoked salmon

100g sliced ham

100g cheddar cheese

2 pickles

3 eggs

some salt

some capers

* See page 4 how to make sushi rice

1 Cut the ham, cheese and pickles into 5mm cubes.

2 Pour the beaten egg and salt in a heated frying pan to make scrambled eggs.

3

Place the sushi rice, ham, cheese, scrambled eggs and pickles in a bowl, mix well, and serve on a plate. Cut the salmon slices in half and then place these on top. Garnish with capers.

• Guide to ingredients - Sushi •

Abura-age	——	fried bean curd – I block refers to 20g (fried tofu)
Benishoga	——	red pickled ginger
Dashi	——	Japanese soup stock
Gari	——	pickled ginger
Gobo	——	burdock root
Kampyo	——	edible gourd
Mirin	——	cooking sake (sweet)
Mochigome	——	Japanese glutinous rice (short grain rice)
Natto	——	fermented soya beans (very strong smell)
Nori	——	sheet of dried seaweed – 'standard size' refers to sheet: 21cm × 19 cm
Renkon	——	lotus root
Shiitake	——	variety of mushroom
Shiso	——	beefsteak plant
Sushi-zu	——	special Japanese vinegar for sushi preparation
Takuan	——	pickled radish
Umeboshi	——	Japanese pickled plums
Wasabi	——	Japanese horseradish